GOOD MORNING, LORD

Devotions on the Hope of Glory

John R. Gunn

BAKER BOOK HOUSE
Grand Rapids, Michigan

ISBN: 0-8010-3706-9

*This Volume Is
Dedicated to Those
in Their Sunset Years*

In a personal message to his family
a year or so before going home, the
author said, "My great desire is to
demonstrate that God goes with us
even down to old age; that His grace
is always sufficient to sustain us."
This faith and trust remained unshaken until the end—no, not the
end—the beginning.

Contents

Foreword

Preface

1. The Ladder Is Still There
   (Genesis 28:12) 11

2. Starless Nights *(Deuteronomy 31:6)* ... 13

3. Will We Know Each Other in Heaven?
   (2 Samuel 12:23) 15

4. The Immortality of the Soul
   (Job 14:14) 17

5. The Light in the Clouds *(Job 37:21)* 19

6. "The Valley of the Shadow of Death"
   (Psalm 23:4) 21

7. This World Is Not Enough
   (Ecclesiastes 3:11) 23

8. Where God Dwells *(Isaiah 60:13)* 25

9. Hold On to Your Faith *(Mark 11:22)* ... 27

10. Easter in Winter *(Mark 16:2)* 29

11. "He Is Risen" *(Luke 24:6)* 31

12. The Life Christ Gives *(John 10:10)* 33

13. Beyond Sight and Sense *(John 14:2)* ... 35

14. Is Heaven a Reality? *(John 14:2)* 37

15. Our Heavenly Home *(John 14:2-3)* 39

16. Peace Nothing Can Destroy
    (John 14:27) 41

17. Angels at the Grave *(John 20:11-12a)* .. 43

18. "Except I Shall See and Put My
    Finger . . ." *(John 20:24-25)* 46

19. Believing Without Seeing *(John 20:29)* . 48

20. More Than Conquerors *(Romans 8:37)* . 51

21. The Answer to Sorrow
    (2 Corinthians 1:3-4) 54

22. A Great Confidence
    (2 Corinthians 4:18) 56

23. When Our Earthly House Falls
    (2 Corinthians 5:1) 58

24. I Am Sure of God *(2 Timothy 1:12)* 60

25. A Faith to Live By and Die By
    (Hebrews 11:1-2, 13) 62

26. Fighting for the Faith *(Jude 3)* 66

27. Able to Keep You *(Jude 24-25)* 71

28. What Lies Beyond?
    (Revelation 1:10-11) 74

29. Faithfulness the Crown of Life
    (Revelation 2:10) 77

30. On to the City of God
    (Revelation 21:1, 2) 79

If you are searching for a deeper spiritual meaning for your life, *Devotions on the Hope of Glory* will point the way. You will indeed benefit in a beautiful and positive manner from these devotionals by minister, author, and newspaper columnist, John R. Gunn.

Pastor Gunn was a former minister in the church I now serve, the First Baptist Church of Fort Wayne, Indiana. It is my pleasure to introduce this volume and to tell you something of its author.

Although John R. Gunn died in 1956 and held his pastorate in Fort Wayne half a century ago during the years 1917 to 1927, the "afterglow" of his ministry is even now a significant spiritual factor in the lives of many people. He had a brilliant mind, was a warm and personable man, stood as a friend ever present in time of need, and emerged as an able leader in the community. In every aspect of his ministry his life reflected the spirit of Jesus Christ.

It is a matter of record that John R. Gunn's greatest service was rendered through his newspaper column, "Short Sermon for Today," published daily by the *Fort Wayne Journal-Gazette*. Unique in the history of American journalism is the fact that the paper continued to carry this daily meditation for fifteen years after his death, for a total newspaper ministry of over fifty years.

Selections for *Devotions on the Hope of Glory* were made from previously published volumes of his newspaper meditations.

Confident that you will find help for your own spiritual needs, I recommend this book to you.

Phillip Philbrook, Pastor
First Baptist Church
Fort Wayne, Indiana

I was happy in my youth and I am still happy. I do not regard my old age as a misfortune; I am enjoying it. God's presence with me makes these sunset years radiant with His love and grace and glory. I am a shut-in. Whittier expresses how I feel about it:

> . . . it [was] well to come
> For deeper rest to this still room
> For here the habit of the soul
> Feels less the outer world's control:
> And from the silence . . .
> The world that time and sense have known
> Falls off and leaves us God alone.

My great desire is to demonstrate that God goes with us even down to old age; that His grace is always sufficient for those who trust Him, sufficient to sustain you in old age. Now that I am old, my great concern is for the younger generation. I want my life in these sunset years to be a testimony to them of what God can mean in a human life. David's prayer in his old age is my prayer:

> Yea, even when I am old and grayheaded, O God, forsake me not; until I have declared thy strength unto the next generation, and thy power to everyone that is to come.

Basic to my philosophy about life in old age is faith in God out of which stems belief in survival after death. I am living as an immortal being, not as one doomed to die and perish in oblivion. The soul cannot be nailed up in a coffin.

The basis of my optimism through life has been my faith in God and trust in His love. That faith and trust remain unshaken. There has been no dimming of my outlook on my life. My faith tells me that the best is yet to be. One of my favorite hymns is "Abide with Me." It was written by Henry Francis Lyte. He was an old man at the time. He was very feeble, and knew he had only a little while to live. I invite you, my friends, especially if like myself you are nearing the end of life's journey, to join with me in the prayer of this hymn:

> Abide with me: fast falls the eventide;
> The darkness deepens; Lord, with me
>   abide!
> When other helpers fail, and comforts flee,
> Help of the helpless, O abide with me.
>
> Swift to its close ebbs out life's little day;
> Earth's joys grow dim, its glories pass
>   away;
> Change and decay in all around I see.
> O Thou, who changest not, abide with me.
>
> Hold Thou Thy cross before my closing
>   eyes;
> Shine through the gloom and point me to
>   the skies;
> Heaven's morning breaks, and earth's vain
>   shadows flee;
> In life, in death, O Lord, abide with me.

John R. Gunn

The Ladder Is Still There

"And he dreamed, and behold a ladder set up on the earth, and the top of it reached to heaven."—*Genesis 28:12.*

On Lincoln's birthday there appeared a striking cartoon in one of our newspapers. A log cabin stood at the base of a high mountain, and on the summit of the mountain rested the White House. Up the steep ascent ran a ladder, with its foot against the cabin and its top reaching the mansion above, and underneath the picture were these words, "The ladder is still there."

The cartoonist, of course, was thinking about the ladder of opportunity. His object was to impress upon the youth of the land that the day of opportunity has not passed. And it has not. The ladder is still there. Especially is that true in this heaven-favored land. But this ladder still calls for hard climbing. It was only by the hardest struggle that Lincoln reached its uppermost round. In his obscure days he said, "I will work hard and some day my opportunity will come." Only thus is it possible to scale this ladder.

But in this message I am thinking of another ladder that is still there, the ladder Jacob saw in his dream, with its foot resting on the earth and its top reaching to heaven. At the top of this ladder is the "mansion of the sky." "In my Father's house are many mansions." The reality of Jacob's dream-ladder is Christ. He is the ladder that reaches from earth to heaven.

Not all the ladders of opportunity are accessible to everybody. But here is a ladder that is accessible to all. And no man can remove it. It was there yesterday, it is still there today, and it will still be there tomorrow. If you miss the ladder to the White House in Washington, there is no reason why you should miss this ladder to the mansion in the sky.

Starless Nights

"Be strong and of a good courage...for the Lord thy God, he it is that doth go with thee; he will not fail thee, nor forsake thee."—Deuteronomy 31:6.

Someone has said, "Blessed is the night, for it reveals to us the stars." It is true that many of us, having passed through such a season, have said: "This has been a blessed night, for it has revealed to me wondrous stars of divine truth and beauty which I had never before seen." But sometimes there are nights when the stars "withdraw their shining." There are periods during which we see not a single ray of light shining through the darkness.

How shall we do in such times? Shall we surrender to the darkness? Shall we give up our trust in God? Let Isaiah speak: "Who is among you that feareth the Lord, that obeyeth the voice of his servant, that walketh in darkness, and hath no light? let him trust in the name of the Lord, and stay upon his God" (50:10).

Listen to the testimony of Paul, in the account of his shipwreck experience: "And when neither sun nor stars in many days appeared, and no small tempest lay on us, all hope that we should be saved was then taken away." Yet, in the face of that dark and apparently hopeless hour, Paul said to the captain and crew of the ship: "Sirs, be of good cheer; for I believe God, that it shall be even as it was told me" (Acts 27:25). God had told Paul that this journey would take him to Rome. The ship might be wrecked, but God's word of promise would ride out the storm!

God does not promise that our way shall always be along a well-lighted road, or that we will sail smooth, calm seas. But He does promise, "I will never leave thee, nor forsake thee." Be of good cheer, you that walk in the night. Even though the stars withdraw their shining, remember God has given His word that He will never leave you, nor forsake you.

Will We Know Each Other in Heaven?

"I shall go to him, but he shall not return to me."
—*2 Samuel 12:23*.

A precious child was dead, and David was in great sorrow. But in his sorrow he comforted his heart with the assurance expressed in the text, "I shall go to him." David believed in a hereafter. He believed that his child was in heaven, that in the end he would go to him there, and that he would recognize and know him as his own dear child.

In literature outside of the Bible, we find this same belief that we shall know our loved ones and friends on the other side. Virgil, in the *Aeneid*, represents Aeneas meeting his father, and describes the tenderness of their greeting. In the *Odyssey*, Homer represents Odysseus in the world beyond, meeting and talking with many whom he had known on earth. Socrates wrote: "What an inconceivable happiness will it be to converse, in another world, with Sisyphus and Odysseus." "O glorious day," cried Cicero, "when I shall retire from this low and sordid scene, to associate with the divine assembly of the departed spirits."

In all ages men universally have believed in a conscious life of mutual recognition in the hereafter. Will this belief be answered with reality? The very fact of its universality is a warrant for regarding it as a prophecy of the truth; for only truth is catholic, while error is sectional. Moreover, it follows from the very nature of the case that, if we live at all in another sphere, we will know each other. Self-consciousness is a characteristic of life, and there can be no consciousness of self without being conscious of others. It follows as a logical sequence that if immortality is a reality heavenly recognition will be a reality.

The Bible leaves no room for doubt concerning this matter. All through the Bible there are glimpses into the heavenly world, and every glimpse into that world reveals the redeemed in blessed and happy companionship. Surely this Book which has taught us so much and so blessed our earthly life, cannot be false in its portrayal of the heavenly life. Unless the Bible misleads us, we shall know each other in heaven. We accept its assurance as positive and certain. And in this assurance we comfort our hearts concerning our precious little ones who have gone from us, and concerning all our departed dear ones and friends who have died in the faith. With a sure confidence, we expect to see them and know them in the world above.

4

The Immortality of the Soul

"If a man die, shall he live again?"—*Job 14:14.*

In the Bible the thought of immortality is translated into the most definite and unmistakable speech. Every page of this blessed old Book gleams with light from the world of a brighter sun. It breathes a spirit perfumed with the fragrance of Paradise.

All the testimony of the Bible gathers around those words of Jesus: "I am the Resurrection and the Life." The resurrection of Christ lies at the bottom of Christianity, and with it the Christian religion stands or falls. Then did Christ rise from the dead? Does He live today? My answer is, if He be not risen, then the grandest factor for good in the world is the result of a huge imposition and deception. If you say that He is not risen, then you make of a lie a force which is conquering heathenism, dethroning vice, exalting virtue, regenerating millions of human lives and leavening the nations with love's sweet influence and the kindly spirit of brotherhood. If He is not risen, from whence sprung the Gospel Tree with its top reaching unto heaven and its branches spreading out over all the bounds of human habitation? The risen Christ is the seed and root of Christianity. Christ lives, and because He lives, His gospel lives, and His church has gathered into her sacred portals redeemed millions whose glad hosannas fill the earth with a chorus of peace and hope and goodwill. Christ lives, the first fruit of the resurrection, and because He lives, we live and shall live forever.

The Light in the Clouds

"Men see not the bright light which is in the clouds."
—*Job 37:21*.

The light in the clouds is a reflection of the sun's light; it means that the sun is still shining; it is a prophecy of another sunrise, the dawn of a new day.

This has a parallel in the realm of human life.

Clouds of trouble and sorrow come over the lives of all of us, but they are not all darkness; there is always a light gleaming through them. The light means that the sun of God's love and goodness is still shining.

"Thy mercy, O Lord, is in the heavens; and thy faithfulness reacheth unto the clouds" (Psalm 36:5).

We too often look only at the shadows the clouds cast upon our way. We look down and see only the darkness they spread around us. That is why "men see not the bright light which is in the clouds."

Look up! The sun is shining somewhere. Look up, and you will see its radiance reflected in those clouds that seem so dark and gloomy.

Sunset means sunrise.

I am now facing life's sunset, but I am looking forward to another sunrise—the dawn of that eternal morning in the land where there shall be no more clouds, no more shadows.

"The Valley of the Shadow of Death"

"Yea though I walk through the valley of the shadow of death, I will fear no evil: for thou art with me; thy rod and thy staff they comfort me."—*Psalm 23:4*.

To our mortal eyes "the valley of the shadow of death" is a place of dismal gloom. But when we approach it, if we can say "Thou art with me," we shall also say "I will fear no evil."

Why should we fear any evil in death? Is it not sent by the hand of the same loving Father that gave us our life? Could He design us evil? Through many of life's valleys He has supported and comforted us with His rod and staff: will He withdraw His support and comfort when we come to death's valley? "If the Lord were pleased to kill us, he would not have . . . showed us all these things, nor . . . told us such things as these" (Judges 13:23). When we think of all the marvelous mercy and lovingkindness God has shown us through life, it is inconceivable that He should abandon us in the end and leave us to perish in Sheol. If He were pleased to do that, then all the blessings we receive from Him in this life are no more than a tantalizing flash. A strange God He would be thus to tantalize us, and then forsake us at last. He is not such a God. His promise, "I will never leave thee nor forsake thee," holds good for our journey through the gloom of the grave, as well as for our journey through this world. After dealing with us during life in the wonderful fashion with which we are so familiar, God will not desert us when we come to the end of the way; He will walk with us still and permit no evil to befall us as we pass through the valley of the shadow of death.

Where there is shadow there is sun; to all valleys there are mountains. Not otherwise is it of death's valley and shadow. Its shadow is but the shadow of our mortality dropping from us as we pass into the light and sun of immortality. Its valley is but a short passage leading to the delectable summits of eternal bliss which lie beyond. It will be but a moment that we are in the shadow. We are not to be detained in the valley; we "walk through" it. And when we come out on the other side, it will be into the sunlight of heaven, where there shall be no more dark valleys; and no more shadows, neither of sorrow, nor sickness, nor death.

This World Is Not Enough

"He hath made everything beautiful in [its] time: also he hath set [eternity] in their heart."—*Ecclesiastes 3:11.*

What a wonderful world is this—"everything beautiful in its time." How appropriately everything is arranged for our enjoyment and delight. How abundant are the provisions made for our temporal needs and comfort. And how multitudinous and varied are the things God has set around us to engage our thought, interest, and activity. In the tiniest flower that blossoms at our feet, there is a wonder and interest which the most diligent scientist can never exhaust.

And yet this world is not enough for man. He has needs which it does not supply. He has faculties for something higher than flowers, faculties which soar beyond the stars. "Also he hath set eternity in their heart." God has endowed man with a capacity for higher researches and activities than those which engage him on the solely mundane level.

One of England's brilliant mathematicians said awhile ago: "I can't feed my soul on mathematics." Mathematical research and teaching were his vocation. He delighted in mathematics, and found therein a vast world of interest to command his endeavor and enthusiasm. But his soul was not satified. Why? Because God, besides giving him a brain for mathematics, had also set eternity in his heart; and the eternal within him reached out after the eternal beyond him.

Beautiful as everything in this world is in its time, man has an eye for a beauty that will not be satisfied until he looks into the face of God and beholds the beauty of His holiness. His heart has been made with a capacity too large for this world to fill, and which cannot be filled "with aught but God, with aught but moral excellence, truth, and love." With eternity in his heart, he can be satisfied only with eternity.

Where God Dwells

"I will make the place of my feet glorious."—*Isaiah 60:13.*

What is it that draws so many tourists
to the Holy Land? Every year for centuries
thousands of pilgrims have traveled across
continents and oceans to visit it. What attracts
them there? It is not any unusual beauty
and charm of scenery in the land. There are
many countries that can boast of far more
wonderful rivers and valleys and mountains.
What, then, is the attraction?

The text answers the question: "I will make
the place of my feet glorious." It was because
Christ walked in Palestine that it has become a
place of glory and fascination. The land derives
its charm, not from the Sea of Galilee, but from
the Man of Galilee. Judea has become the most
immortal of nations because it was "the place
of God's feet." Her prophets and kings, her
palaces and temples, her literature and laws,
her music and songs, her rivers, lakes, hills,
and valleys, her whole existence and history,
all relate to God and religion. Because the Divine Presence dwelt there, Palestine is the
spiritual mecca of mankind.

And herein is a parable for us. We, too, can
make the place of our feet hallowed, if we will

but walk by the will of God and in step with Him. We may have all the disadvantages of Judea—isolation, narrow limitations, unattractive environment—and yet, if we will permit God to dwell in our hearts and live in our lives, it will mean the glorifying and hallowing of the sphere wherein our feet are placed. All places and spheres become glorious—*where God dwells*.

"Hold On to Your Faith"

"Have faith in God."—*Mark 11:22.*

The word Jesus used was *Exete,* which means "hold on to." When He said, *"Exete* faith in God," His disciples understood Him to mean, "Hold on to your faith in God."

We are often tempted to let go our faith and to doubt, just as we are tempted in other directions. Sometimes this temptation arises from intellectual perplexities. But perhaps more often it arises from experiences that perplex and bewilder us. Trouble or sorrow comes; we are puzzled, and wonder why it should be so; doubt assails us, our faith is shaken, and we are tempted to give up altogether our belief in God and religion.

Let us not think it strange when we are so tempted. We should regard it as we regard any other temptation. We should resist it, just as we resist temptation to commit positive evil. That we are so tempted is no more strange than any of the other common temptations of life.

"Hold on to your faith." You would not let the demon of vice rob you of your virtue. You would not suffer the demon of covetousness to rob you of your honor. Be just as determined not to allow the demon of doubt to rob you of your faith. Guard your faith just as jealously as you guard your virtue and honor.

You will have your trials and disappointments, just as everybody else. But when these come, and when fears and doubts assail you, stick to your faith. Do that, and you may be sure God will stick to you. God does not promise that your way shall always be along a sunlit road, that you shall never walk the dark ways of life; but He does promise this; "My presence shall go with thee."

"In the world ye shall have tribulation." There is no escape from that. But "faith is the victory that overcomes the world"—and the *only* victory that overcomes the world. All along there are world forces operating against us which only faith can master and overcome. Ultimately the world removes from us all the outward things upon which we build our lives, when all that is left to us is our faith in God and the hope built on that faith. Therefore, though a thousand tragedies befall you, whatever sorrows or losses you may suffer—*hold on to your faith in God.*

Easter in Winter

"They came to the sepulchre at the rising of the sun."
—Mark 16:2.

When they came to the tomb they found a surprising thing—the tomb was empty!

A spring sunrise. Resurrection and new life—the Easter message.

We need the Easter message in winter as much as in the spring, if not more. In the spring we see all nature bursting forth into new life. The resurrection of life in nature helps us to believe in the resurrection of human life.

It is different in winter—the trees stripped of their leaves, bleakness and barrenness everywhere, nothing to suggest resurrection and new life.

Many of us have had a loved one pass away in wintry weather. We take the body on a cold winter day and lay it in a cold grave. We are left stunned, brokenhearted, with an empty, lonely feeling.

We return home and wander aimlessly in the broken household. Out of the depths of our heart we cry with Job, "If a man die, shall he live again?" Then, like the sun breaking through the clouds and lighting up a dark winter day, comes that hope-inspiring declaration of Christ: "I am the resurrection, and the life: he that believeth on me, though he were dead, yet shall he live; and whosoever liveth and believeth on me shall never die" (John 11:25-26).

After Christ was buried in the tomb, the last word was death. After Easter, the last word is life. Life—not death. Not annihilation but everlasting life, not the end of day but day-break, not the gloom of winter but the gladness of spring, not exit but entrance, entrance into the Father's house.

Easter changed shame to glory, fear to faith, despair to gladness, sunset to sunrise.

To the penitent man who died by His side on the cross Christ said, "Today shalt thou be with me in paradise" (Luke 23:43). On that day they met and recognized each other in paradise. This means that all of us who know the love of Christ shall recognize our loved ones in heaven. The loved one you have lost in death is lost only for a while. The promise from Jesus is reassuring: "I go to prepare a place for you . . . that where I am, you may be also" (John 14:3, RSV).

"He Is Risen"

"He is not here, but is risen."—*Luke 24:6.*

"He is not here"—in the tomb. No crypt can hold Him! A floor of rock, a roof of rock, a wall of rock, a door of rock, the seal of the Sanhedrin, a regiment of Roman soldiers, cannot keep Christ in the sepulcher. Men may entomb Him in their creeds and traditions, but He lifts the door from its hinges and flings it flat in the dust. Men may pile upon Him their hatreds and animosities, and all manner of opposition and obstruction, but He overthrows the whole pile and tramples it beneath His conquering feet.

"He is not here"—and neither is the cause for which He died bound here in the tomb of death. He died to redeem a fallen race, and in spite of all the powers of darkness and evil the work of redemption goes on! The Christian religion cannot be put down. Not all the ignorance and superstition and persecution that were arrayed against Christianity in the "dark ages" were enough to destroy it. Men are always digging graves in which to bury Christianity, but it refuses to be buried. They may from time to time accomplish its partial entombment, but out of every such entombment it breaks forth into new life and power, and goes marching on, conquering and to conquer.

"He is not here, but is risen." Risen! Christ risen!—the most signal event of all history. It was an event that signaled the triumph of life over death, truth over falsehood, right over wrong, love over hate, light over darkness. Death and darkness, and all their forces— malice, hate, error, injustice, and wrong—stand as defeated and conquered foes. The forces of light and life—truth, righteousness, love, peace, and goodwill—are the conquering forces of the world. There are no tombs in which they can be sealed up and held. There are no grave-clothes stout enough to bind them and hold them down. Let them be crushed to the earth as often as men will, but they rise again and again; the eternal years of God are theirs.

"He is risen"—and with Him is risen a new race, "a chosen generation, a royal priesthood, an holy nation, a peculiar people, who show forth the praises of him who called them out of darkness into his marvelous light," and of whom it is said, "They shall not be confounded." There are no "gates of hell" that can confound them or prevail against them as they go forth in the name and power of the risen Christ to establish in the world His kingdom over which He shall reign as *King of kings and Lord of lords*.

The Life Christ Gives

"I am come that they might have life, and that they might
have it more abundantly."—*John 10:10*.

In the midst of the colorful age in which we
live, there is nothing that people dread so much
as a dull and colorless life. The great desire
today is for life and action. People want to appear vivacious and lively; and to that end they
are continually turning to one thing and
another, to external sources, seeking something that will stimulate them, something that
will thrill and excite them, something that will
compel enthusiasm and movement. The result
is that much of the life and action we see today
is artificial. People are not really living; they
are only existing on a drug-stimulated vitality.

The real life is the Christian life. And the
secret of the Christian life lies here, in the
promise of Christ: "I am come that they might
have life, and that they might have it more
abundantly." We are so familiar with this
promise that we miss a great deal of it. Turn life
into vitality, and see if it suggests more. We
know people of overflowing vitality, who not
only exist but live—live adventurously, joy-
ously, abundantly. And so living, they radiate
life into everybody they meet and every object

they touch. Can Christ's promise mean less than that, a duller life? Some have pictured Christ as dull and colorless, but that representation of Him is false. His was the most colorful life ever lived in this world. And it is His own life that He imparts to us. "In him was life, and the life was the light of men." "The bread of God is he which cometh down from heaven, and giveth life unto the world."

The man who really lives is the man made alive by the life Christ gives. He does not have to look to external sources to keep himself alive and going. He is not dependent upon artificial stimulants—stimulants that soon lose their power to stimulate, making it necessary to seek others. "Whosoever drinketh of the water that I shall give him shall never thirst; but the water that I shall give him shall be in him a well of water springing up into everlasting life." There is no ebb and flow in the life that comes from Christ.

Everywhere today people are saying, "We want life; we want life abundant; we want spirit and color and movement." Let them take Christ, and they will have what they want and seek. If people would escape the dull and stale effects of artificial living; if they want life full of vitality and sustaining interests, let them seek and receive—the life Christ gives.

Beyond Sight and Sense

"In my Father's house are many mansions." —*John 14:2*.

On one occasion Sir Oliver Lodge, the great scientist, was speaking on the immensity and magnificence of the universe. In the course of his address he paused, and with a deepened intensity in his voice, said: "Have no fear, there is no rightful demand you can make upon this universe that it will not fulfill."

The Christian faith affirms that we live in a universe that is a house of many mansions. What we see of it is but a small part of what there is to see. Beyond the frontiers of sight and sense lies a spiritual realm infinite in its reaches and inexhaustible in its riches. Much of what is there must seem puzzling from this side, and many of our eager questions must go unanswered. But, returning to Sir Oliver Lodge's statement about the physical universe, there is no rightful expectation we can have toward the spiritual universe that it will not fulfill.

At the end of life's journey we come to what appears to our mortal sense to be a terminus. We call it death. The Christian faith says that death is not a terminus, that it is but passing through a dark entry, out of one little dusky room of the Father's house into another that is fair and large, lightsome and glorious—one that will fulfill our highest expectations. Think of going to sleep and waking up in such a room. That, says the Christian faith, is death.

We sometimes congratulate ourselves at the moment of waking from a troubled dream. It may be so the moment after death.

> Just think
> Of stepping on shore
> And finding it Heaven;
> Of taking hold of a hand
> And finding it God's hand;
> Of breathing a new air
> And finding it celestial air;
> Of feeling invigorated
> And finding it immortality;
> Of passing from storm and
> Tempest to an unbroken calm;
> Of waking up—and
> Finding it Home!
>   (Author unknown)

Is Heaven a Reality?

"In my Father's house are many mansions: if it were not so, I would have told you." —*John 14:2*.

In a recent magazine article, discussing what the religion of the future would be, the writer said, among other things, that the idea of heaven would have no place in the religion of the future. Evidently this writer thinks that the notion of heaven is only a superstition handed down by tradition, and that eventually it will be outgrown as the world advances in education and enlightenment. But the world is already a good many thousand years old, and from the beginning men of every race and clime have dreamed of a heaven above, and have lived in the hope and expectation of going there when this life was ended. And still they go on dreaming the same thing and living in the same hope and expectation. The idea of heaven is just as deep seated in the thought of men today as ever, and just as universal. There does not seem to be any indication that the idea is playing out. And in view of the fact that it has persisted through all the ages and in every age held the hearts of men so universally, who can believe that it is only a superstition and that it will have no place in the religion of the future?

If the religion of the future has no heaven in it, it will be a poor religion. It will not answer to the deepest longings and aspirations of the human heart. It will not be based on the Bible, for the Bible has much to say about heaven and leads us to believe that it is a reality. Then we have the testimony of many saints in their dying hour, when the veil that separates the seen from the unseen was drawn aside and they talked of what they saw beyond. When Moody came to die, he said to his son, just a few hours before passing away, "I have had a vision; God has let me look into another world; earth is receding, heaven is opening up." Moody was a cool-headed, sane, practical man, and not the kind to be deceived in such a matter. I believe God let him, and the many others from whom we have had similar words in their last moments, look into the beyond and talk of what they saw, just to reassure us.

God be praised for the hope of heaven. To be robbed of this blessed hope would leave us poor indeed.

Our Heavenly Home

"In my Father's house are many mansions; if it were not
so, I would have told you. I go to prepare a place for you.
And if I go and prepare a place for you, I will come again,
and receive you unto myself; that where I am, there ye may
be also."—*John 14:2-3*.

Jesus said, "I go to prepare a place for you."
He said, "In my Father's house are many mansions; if it were not so, I would have told you."
Do you think that Jesus, who loved us and gave
Himself to die for us, would deceive us about
such a matter? I know He would not. If heaven
were not a reality, He would have told us so.
There is nothing anywhere in the Bible convey-
ing the idea that heaven is not a reality and not
a place. On the other hand, everything in the
Bible in regard to heaven leads us to believe
that it is a *real place*.

Then we have the convincing testimony of
many saints in their dying hour, when the veil
that separates the seen from the unseen was
drawn aside and they talked of what they saw
in the glory land. Adams, the great missionary
to West Africa, said in his dying hour, "I see
glorious sights! I see heaven! Let me go! I want
no more of earth." Edward Payson, when on
his dying bed, said, "The Celestial City is in
full view, its glories beam upon me, its music

strikes upon my ear and its spirit breathes into my heart.''

These men were not the kind of men to be deceived. Their testimonies lead us to believe that heaven is one of the most certain realities. I believe that God let them look into the future and speak thus of what they saw to strengthen and help us. These things ought to inspire us and cause us to quicken our steps as we journey toward our home in heaven.

I love to think of John's vision when he saw the saints gathered into the "tabernacle of God," when "He shall wipe away every tear from their eyes; and death shall be no more: neither shall there be mourning, nor crying, nor pain, any more." In the midst of this world of sin and death, what a blessed hope is this! Sometime ago a young man lay dying. His heart saddened by the thought of leaving his loved ones, his eyes had become wet with weeping. A minister sat by his bedside and wiped away the tears. As he did so the young man looked up at him and said, "Doctor, the next time the tears are wiped from my eyes, it will be by the hand of God."

Peace Nothing Can Destroy

"My peace I give unto you: not as the world giveth, give I
unto you."—*John 14:27*

The world may give you things that will
make you feel at ease, and so at peace. But you
can lose those things, and then your feeling of
ease will be gone, and the peace that feeling
gave you will be turned into anguish and
bitterness.

The peace Christ gives is His peace—"My
peace I give to you." He was poor, had not
where to lay His head (Luke 9:58). But poverty
didn't disturb His peace. He was hated and
crucified, but that didn't break His peace. He
died, saying, "Father, into thy hands I commend
my spirit" (Luke 23:46). The source of His
peace was trust in the heavenly Father, the
doing of His will, the consciousness that there
was nothing between Him and the Father. And
that is the peace He gives us. He removes the
barrier of sin that separates us from the Father,
and brings us into a trustful and obedient relationship with Him. Thus, the source of His
peace becomes the source of our peace.

This is peace which the world can neither
give nor take away.

After His resurrection Christ appeared to the

disciples, and said to them, "Peace be unto you" (John 20:19). The words had back of them the power and authority of His resurrection. He had defeated all the forces which destroy the peace of men. The disciples were in great fear because of the hostility that encompassed them, the self-same hostility which had encompassed His death. Now, having overcome death, He said, "Peace be unto you." It was as though He said: "The things you fear cannot harm you. Death is not the end—behold me alive! Be at peace, for whether in life or death you are safe."

He then showed them the crucifixion wounds in His hands and in His side, so that there might be no doubt in their minds that He was the Lord. And then He repeated the same words, prefacing a commission: "Peace be unto you; as the Father hath sent me, even so send I you" (v. 21). They were to be sent as He had been sent, to accomplish the Father's will and purpose. By the fact of His resurrection, they could be at peace and assured of being victorious in their mission, even though they went His way of suffering and death.

The peace Christ gives is abiding—peace nothing can destroy.

Angels at the Grave

"Mary stood without at the sepulchre weeping: and as she wept, she stooped down, and looked into the sepulchre, and seeth two angels."—*John 20:11-12a.*

It was the morning of the first Easter. Mary had gone into the garden to visit the tomb of Jesus. As she stood there beside the tomb she saw two angels. These angels were messengers from heaven, come to bring her a message of cheer and hope. Seeing them and hearing them say, "He is not here but is risen," a great and unspeakable comfort passed into her heart.

Experiences something like this are not uncommon to us. As Mary saw angels at the grave of Him she loved, so do we see them as we stand at the graveside of those we love. There, in the midst of the dark night of death, "hope sees a star, and listening love can hear the rustle of a wing."

I can never forget when I stood beside the grave of my firstborn, who passed away at the age of two years. My heart was crushed with grief. But through my tears I seemed to see an angel from heaven; and I heard a voice as the voice of an angel, singing:

Safe in the arms of Jesus
Safe on His gentle breast,

> There by His love o'er shaded
> Sweetly his soul doth rest.

Once again, a little while ago, I stood by another grave—that which covered from my sight all that was mortal of my precious mother. From childhood she had been the angel of my life. As I stood there and held in my vision her familiar form, that form became transfigured into the form of an angel; and I heard her voice as that of an angel; and I seemed to hear her singing, as I had many times before heard her sing:

> At the feet of my Redeemer
> Would I breathe my latest breath,
> Then by angel guards attended
> Wing my flight to worlds on high.

Even Colonel Ingersol, when he stood at the graveside of his brother, heard the rustle of an angel's wing and gave expression to a glimmering hope of immortality. The same was true of the unbelieving Hume at his mother's grave. As he thought of her beautiful soul, she seemed to appear before him as a glorified angel; and he could not but feel that she was still living. We all have the same feeling when we think of any pure and noble soul who has departed this life. When we stand at the graveside of those we have loved and in whom we have recognized the virtues of true character, we feel that they must still live and must still be expressing somewhere and somehow their Godlike qualities and heavenlike ideals. No wonder angels from the unseen world come to us. They come from God to reassure us and to call us to the blessed hope of the life beyond. And how our hearts are comforted by these angels who greet us at the grave.

"Except I Shall See and Put My Finger . . ."

"But Thomas, one of the twelve, called Didymus, was not with them when Jesus came. The other disciples therefore said unto him, We have seen the Lord. But he said unto them, Except I shall see in his hands the print of the nails, and put my finger into the print of the nails, and thrust my hand into his side, I will not believe."—*John 20:24-25*.

"You tell me that Jesus is risen, that you have seen Him. I cannot believe such a thing; it seems too unreal. Before I will be convinced, I must see for myself; I must even see the print of the nails in His hands; more than that, I must put my finger into the print of the nails, and thrust my hand into the spear wound in His side. I will not believe—*except I shall see and put my finger in.*"

That was Thomas. He would not believe what he could not see. He would not even believe his eyes; he put his faith only in his hands. Later, being cured of his scepticism, he declined the material test he had demanded, fell down in the presence of Jesus, and joyfully exclaimed, "My Lord and my God!" But for the time being he was a materialist; he would not rely on anything but material certainties and consolations—such things as his eyes could see and his hands could touch.

The world is full of Thomases today; men

who refuse credence to all spiritual concepts, and who place reliance only on things that are tangible to their bodily senses. Talk to these men about the resurrection of Christ and its spiritual significance, and they assume the Thomas attitude, "Except I shall see and put my finger. . . ." The spiritualities of life mean nothing to them; to their minds such things are too unreal to be of practical value. The "real things" are such things as minister to their physical appetites and comfort, worldly ambitions and vanities. They believe in the "solid earth"; all above the earth is as "the unsubstantial islands of the clouds." Like Thomas, they have only a "hand" faith, and they decline to believe any gospel that does not put something into their hands.

"Blessed are they that have not seen, and yet have believed." The deepest things of life are spiritual things, "which the eyes of the flesh cannot see and the hands of the flesh cannot handle," but which reach the soul directly—and only the soul opens to receive them. The man who says, "Except I shall see and put my finger . . ." has his soul locked shut and cannot receive them; and until he opens his soul he will never perceive the spiritual presences and significances with which God's world is filled; he will never see the risen Christ and realize the joy of saying to Him, "My Lord and my God."

19

Believing Without Seeing

"Blessed are they that have not seen, and yet have believed."
—*John 20:29*.

This is one of the sayings of Jesus. By it He does not mean to put a premium upon credulity. He is not pronouncing a benediction upon those who believe without reason. God has endowed man with the power to reason, and Jesus would not discredit that power by extolling blind credulity.

In religion, as well as elsewhere, we should use our reason. The apostle Peter urges that we be ready to give a reason for the hope that is in us. Religion has no propositions that we are called upon to accept without reasonable grounds. But what constitutes a reasonable ground for believing and accepting a proposition? Does reason forbid faith in the unseen? Physical sight may aid faith, but it is not essential to it. The deepest truths are spiritual truths, which the eyes of the flesh cannot see and the hands of the flesh cannot handle. It was with this conception that Jesus spoke when He pronounced a special blessing upon those who believe without seeing.

The Christian religion presents to us Jesus Christ, calls upon us to believe the whole New

Testament story about Him, to accept Him for what He claimed to be, and to crown Him as our Savior and Lord. We never saw Jesus in the flesh. We were not witnesses to His miracles. It has not been given to us, as to Thomas, to see the nail prints in His hands, verifying His resurrection from the dead. How can we believe that He ever lived? How can we accept the testimony the New Testament bears concerning Him? Do we say that not having seen Him, and not having witnessed the events related of Him, we will not believe? Do we, like Thomas, demand to see and handle the body of His flesh before we will believe and accept Him?

Archbishop Whately wrote a book on *Historic Doubts Concerning Napoleon Bonaparte* and many people were convinced by the book that no such person as Napoleon Bonaparte ever existed. The clever Archbishop did this with two things in view: to show that the strongest evidence could be distorted and discounted, and to show the absurdity of denying credence to things beyond our sight and touch. It was a rebuke to the doubting Thomases who demand physical sight and touch as a condition of faith, to men who will not believe the overwhelming evidence that Jesus was what He claimed to be and ought to be taken into their lives as divine Redeemer and Lord.

We are glad for the testimony of those who saw Jesus in the flesh and witnessed the events of His earthly life. But he who believes on Him without seeing becomes the recipient of all the blessings that came to those who saw. Yea, a special blessedness is promised to those who have not seen, and yet believe. They have a more sure foundation for their faith and hope than the evidences that rest upon the perishable substance of physical and material things. "The things which are seen are temporal, but the things which are not seen are eternal."

More Than Conquerors

"In all these things we are more than conquerors."
— *Romans 8:37.*

The greatest conquerors are not the Genghis Khans, the Attillas, the Alexanders, the Napoleons; they are those who conquer themselves, who are masters of their own souls. "Greater is he that ruleth his spirit than he that taketh a city."

We talk about this and that way of life; there is just one life for which one is wholly responsible and whose way he can alter, and that life is his own. If you want to help build a better way of life for mankind, you must begin with your own life. If you want to help subdue the evils in the world, you should first subdue the evils in your own soul. The first and most important conquest to which life challenges us, is the conquest of ourselves.

The conquering of ourselves leads on to other conquests; we have to go on to conquer the evils and perils that beset us from without. It is through the indwelling of Christ and the power of His love in our hearts that self is conquered. And through Him we are made more than conquerors over the world and all the foes it is able to marshal against us.

"What can ever part us from Christ's love? Can anguish or calamity or persecution or famine or nakedness or danger or the sword? No, in all this we are more than conquerors through him who loved us" (Romans 8:35, 37, Moffatt).

To conquer is to subdue, to master, to overcome, in the sense of defeating an attack. To conquer anguish is to overcome it and replace it with joy. To conquer peril is to defeat it and secure safety.

This is conquering that makes us more than conquerors. We do more than repel the assaults of evil; we make them contribute to the strengthening of our character and the enrichment of our lives. We do more than overcome our trials and tribulations; we wrest from them values that could never be gained otherwise than through the struggle we make against them. Experiencing anguish, we are having fellowship with the suffering which uplifts and beautifies life. Bearing persecution, we are demonstrating the meaning of true godliness, and learning what Jesus meant when He said: "Blessed are those who have been persecuted for the sake of goodness! The realm of heaven is theirs" (Matthew 5:10, Moffatt). Facing and overcoming perils, we are revealing the power of our Savior and Lord and sharing the majesty of His power.

What of the sword? Can that death-dealing weapon part us from Christ's love? No, in this also, Paul says, we are more than conquerors through Him who loved us.

Translated into Christ's language, the word *death* means "life"! Going out into life, a life of eternal youth, a life free from the bounds of sense and time—that is dying in the meaning of the Christian faith. "O death, where is your victory? The victory is ours, thank God! He makes it ours by our Lord Jesus Christ" (1 Corinthians 15:55, 57, Moffatt).

21

The Answer to Sorrow

"Blessed be the God and Father of our Lord Jesus Christ, the Father of tender mercies and the God of all comfort, who comforts me in all my affliction, so that I am able to comfort people who are in any distress by the comfort with which I myself am comforted by God."
—*2 Corinthians 1:3-4 (Moffatt)*.

A friend has lost a loved one. You want so much to comfort that friend. What can you say? You can't change the fact of death. You try to console. You send flowers. This helps— but it does not heal the broken heart. After all you say and do, the heart still grieves. There *is* an answer to sorrow. The answer is faith. It is *the only* answer, if the bereft one is to accept the cruel decree and find a spirit strong enough to pick up the broken threads and go on to live with a brave heart.

The faith a broken heart must have is that faith that looks through tear-filled eyes and reaches up a helpless hand to the strong hand of God, "the Father of mercies and God of all comfort."

Grief never finds its solace in words of comfort spoken by friends. No friends, no minister, can still the sobbing heart of a bereft one. The bereaved one must minister to his own wounds, must lift his own lantern of faith and walk in the light that shines from the inside—a lantern lighted by Him who said, "Let not your heart be troubled; ye believe in God, believe also in me. In my Father's house are many mansions; if it were not so, I would have told you. I go to prepare a place for you. And if I go and prepare a place for you, I will come again, and will receive you unto myself; that where I am, there ye may be also."

There is something radiant in this truth—so radiant that if grieving hearts will lay hold of it, the sunshine will break through the clouds and light the way.

22

A Great Confidence

"The seen is transient, the unseen eternal."
—*2 Corinthians 4:18 (Moffatt).*

Unseen things—they are the great realities, the ultimate things of life. Because Paul had his eyes fixed on these things, he could say: "I never lose heart; though my outward man decays, my inner man is renewed day after day. The slight trouble of the passing hour results in a solid glory past all comparison, for those of us whose eyes are on the unseen" (vv. 16-18, Moffatt). In the next verse he declares: "I know that if this earthly tent of mine is taken down, I get a home from God, made by no human hands, eternal in the heavens" (5:1, Moffatt).

Here was a far view. Paul set his thinking in the large context of eternity. He looked beyond the trials and sufferings of this present time; saw past them an eternal heritage which they could not spoil. This view and its concomitant faith inspired in him a great confidence—a confidence that rested not on the transient things of earth, but on the eternal verities.

The man who has this confidence has something that will save him from pessimism and the bitter feeling of futility; something that will make him feel that life is good and worth living;

something that will give him the stamina to endure reverses and disappointments without losing heart; something that will sustain him in time of trial and trouble, in the hour of affliction and sorrow; something that will keep his heart up when the times are dark and desperate; something that will inspire him to high and noble endeavor and make him a dynamic power for good; something that will keep him going and keep a song in his heart in life's darkest hours; something that will take away the fear of death and enable him to approach the grave in the joy of victory.

The secret of great and triumphant living lies in being related to the ultimate things of life— the things which link us to God and the eternal. The bodies we love and the things we have made with our hands are destined for the dust. Seeing everything about us changing and going back to the original elements, it is reassuring and inspiring to know that the invisible world is not conditioned by time nor affected by it. To make life worthwhile, we must, by faith, be linked with that world and live as immortals.

23

When Our Earthly House Falls

"For we know that if our earthly house of this tabernacle were dissolved, we have a building of God, an house not made with hands, eternal in the heavens."
—2 Corinthians 5:1.

John Quincy Adams at the age of eighty was walking down the streets of Boston one day when he met an old friend who shook his trembling hand, and said, "Good-morning, how is John Quincy Adams today?" "Thank you," the ex-president answered, "John Quincy Adams is quite well, quite well, I thank you. But the house in which he lives at present is becoming dilapidated. It is tottering upon its foundation. Time and seasons have nearly destroyed it. Its roof is pretty well worn out. Its walls are much shattered, and it trembles with every wind. The old tenement is almost uninhabitable, and I think John Quincy Adams will have to move out of it soon."

Sooner or later we all come to the time when we realize that our earthly house is tottering. The body is wonderfully made, but it cannot forever withstand the ravages of time and wear. This house of clay in which I live has weathered many storms; it has stood up well under the usage of a good many years; but after a while it is going to fail, and I will have to move out of it.

When this moving time comes I want to be sure that I have another house ready and waiting for me. Where shall I look for that house? What kind of house will it be? The answer is here in the words of the great apostle: "For we know that if our earthly house of this tabernacle were dissolved, we have a building of God, an house not made with hands, eternal in the heavens." This answer satisfies me as to the place of my future abode. I have not seen the house, and there is little I can tell you about its location. But it is of God's building, and is located somewhere in His holy heaven; and that's enough for me. When the time comes to move into it I know I shall not be disappointed. I shall move into it with rejoicing—when my earthly house fails.

24

I Am Sure of God

"I know whom I have trusted, and I am certain that he is able to keep what I have put into his hands, till the great day."—*2 Timothy 1:12 (Moffatt).*

Someone asked Robert Browning whether, in all the poetry he had written, there were any lines which expressed in a few words all that was fundamental to his thought and life. He said, "Yes," and quoted the lines: "He at least believed in soul, Was very sure of God."

It is a great thing to be able to say that you are sure of God. The man who is able to say this, without any faltering of voice, has a confidence nothing can shake, a peace nothing can disturb. It is because men do not believe in God with a sure and certain confidence, that they fret over the misfortunes of today, and are worried about what may happen tomorrow.

I take my stand with Browning—I am sure of God.

Being sure of God—what?

1. I cast all my anxieties on Him, in the confidence that His great interest is in me (1 Peter 5:7, Moffatt).

2. I know He will make all things work together for my good, in accordance with His purpose of love (Romans 8:28).

3. I am content to leave with Him the care of my life, "certain that he is able to keep what I have put into his hands."

4. I am not afraid of death. "God will redeem my soul from the power of Sheol; for he will receive me" (Psalm 49:15). "O death where is your victory? The victory is ours, thank God! He makes it ours by our Lord Jesus Christ" (1 Corinthians 15:57, Moffatt).

5. I have all confidence in the triumph of right over wrong, truth over falsehood, love over hate. "Though the wrong seems oft so strong, God is the Ruler yet. . . . The battle is not done, Jesus who died shall be satisfied, and earth and heav'n be one."

6. I do not trouble my mind over things beyond my comprehension. "Lord, my heart is not haughty, nor mine eyes lofty: neither do I exercise myself in great matters, or in things too high for me. Surely I have . . . quieted myself" (Psalm 131:1-2).

25

A Faith to Live By and Die By

"Now faith means that we are confident of what we hope for, convinced of what we do not see. It was for this that the men of old won their record. . . . These all died in the faith."—*Hebrews 11:1-2, 13 (Moffatt)*.

For many years I have tried to follow and teach the philosophy of life contained in the Bible. However, the Bible is not a book of philosophy; it is rather a book of life. Instead of a philosophy in the conventional sense, it provides us with living commentaries on the business of living. Within the pages of the Bible, we see men and women living and moving in the midst of the world, entering into all the experiences of life as we ourselves know them. We see some of these men and women go down in defeat, and we can hardly miss seeing why. Some of them are victorious, and the secret of their victory is plainly revealed. You see what I mean, when I say that the Bible gives us living commentaries on the business of living.

There are resources for living, resources which enable one to live triumphantly. What are those resources? For the answer to that question, we want something more than a philosophy, something more than a theory; we want living testimonies. And we have such testimonies in the lives of Enoch, Noah, Abraham, Moses, and all the great and good men who move before us in the pages of the Bible. One word gives us the key to their lives —faith. Faith in God. Faith in things unseen and eternal. By faith they laid hold of God. Through prayer they communed with the Infinite. Out of that relationship came the resources by which they lived and conquered.

The faith that made these great characters in the Bible has been the faith of countless millions of people. In all times and all climes men have been intuitively aware of "things not seen," of spiritual resources not perceptible to the physical senses, and by faith they have acted on the conviction of the reality of the unseen. And believing souls have made this faith a working principle of life. By its power they have mastered their doubts and terrors, overcome their trials and troubles, conquered their difficulties, lived triumphant lives, and achieved the noblest ends in practical accomplishment.

These believing souls died in the faith they had lived by—died as triumphantly as they had lived. For them, death had no terrors. They believed the saying of Scripture, "Death is swallowed up in victory." Across the ages comes that word of faith from Israel's immortal singer: "Yea, though I walk through the valley of the shadow of death, I will fear no evil: for thou art with me; thy rod and thy staff they comfort me." And down the centuries rings

Paul's shout: "O Death, where is your victory? O Death, where is your sting? The victory is ours, thank God! He makes it ours by our Lord Jesus Christ" (1 Corinthians 15:55, 57).

Faith has a history. One page from its history which I came across some while ago, was written by an American soldier in France, just before he died in a field hospital. It was a letter to his father. Before he went to France, he had lost his mother and his wife. An old hymn, learned as a child at the knee of the father who reared him after his mother's death, eased the bitterness of parting for this soldier. He wrote:

Dear Dad:
Do you remember how you used to hold me on your knee and sing:

> When the final farewell to the
> world I have said,
> And gladly lie down to my rest?

It took me a long time to learn it all, but the first time I heard it I remembered the last two lines:

> Will any one there at the
> beautiful gate
> Be watching and waiting for me?

I am so glad to know that mother and wife will both be there at the gate waiting and watching for me.

My hour has come, Dad, and I want to thank you for being such a wonderful father. You had to be both father and mother to me. I don't think even mother could have been a gentler guide and counselor than you were. I'll sure tell her how you loved her memory. I am glad you instilled your faith in me and showed me by example how to live a Christian life. It is my support now, as I am starting down the valley of the shadow. My heart nearly broke when Claire left us and I almost cursed God for robbing me of my wife. Your consolation then saved my reason. May God bless you as you deserve for all your goodness and kindness, although you had your own cross to bear. I will meet mother and Claire a far different man than I would have been but for you.

Good-by, Dad, until we meet again.

Robert

This soldier's faith was that faith which has been man's salvation through the ages. This is the faith I want and you want—a faith to live by and die by.

26

Fighting for the Faith

"Go on strongly fighting for the faith which has been given to the saints once and for ever."—*Jude 3 (N. T. in Basic English)*.

A final word should be said by way of emphasizing the importance to modern Christendom of its appeal in behalf of the faith which was once for all committed to the saints. The institutions of Christendom rest upon that faith. If that faith should perish, these institutions would perish, and Christendom would revert to paganism.

The hope of the world depends upon the outcome of this battle; and how the battle goes depends upon our response to Jude's appeal: "Go on strongly fighting for the faith." Mark well the words, "strongly fighting." A halfhearted, halfway fight will not do. Nor will it do merely to defend our position; we must go on to challenge paganism in all of its strongholds.

The only way to combat secularism and the atheistic ideologies that spring therefrom is to practice Christianity. We must make our supreme commitment to the spiritual forces of life. We must make it our chief business to seek first the kingdom of God and His righteousness, remembering Christ's words, "Do not be troubled, and cry, 'What are we to eat?' or 'what are we to drink?' or 'how are we to be clothed?' for well your heavenly Father knows you need all that." Pagans make all that their aim in life, Jesus says. We Christians are not to be like that. Trust your heavenly Father, Jesus says; seek the kingdom of God and all these things will be added unto you. This is not to be taken as an assurance that we shall never lack these things. Did not Jesus say that those who enter His service must be prepared to endure privation and hardship? How then are we to take this assurance? For its full and ultimate meaning, we must look beyond the narrow context of our immediate personal needs and interpret it in the larger context of society as a whole. The world is always troubled about the bread problem, the clothing problem—problems relating to material and temporal needs. Jesus was pointing to the solution of these problems, when He said: "Seek ye first the kingdom of God and His righteousness, and all these things shall be added unto you."

One cannot say that America is exactly a Christian nation. But we are a nation built on and committed to Christian ideals. And today we are being challenged to show the world that our way of life offers the best hope to mankind. The Russian people are committed to Soviet ideology, which is based on a materialistic doctrine. Their philosophy has its appeal, it offers something tangible, something you can put your hands on. We've got to make our philosophy tangible, too. We've got to show the people of the world with material values how Christianity works for their well-being. We've got to counter the materialistic appeal of the Soviets with the appeal of material values produced by the practice of Christian ideals. But we must not magnify material values out of proportion. We must not forget, and not let the world forget, the truth Christ enunciated, when He said to the multitudes who had been following Him because He fed them with loaves and fishes: "I am the living bread that comes down from heaven. He who feeds on me will also live by me. What gives life is the Spirit. The words I have uttered to you are spirit and life."

The time of test is here for Christendom. If we are going to put up any sort of fight, there must be no hesitancy, no drawing back. We must be done with vague and shallow thinking. We must make up our minds about Christ; we must be fully persuaded in our own minds concerning Him and what He stands for, and concerning the worth and power of His gospel. Unfortunately there is something in the taunt occasionally thrown at us, that we do not go about the business of Christianity as though fully persuaded of its importance. The lukewarm support many give to the church is a tacit admission that the church is not so very vital after all.

We who are of Christendom need to do some rethinking about Christ and Christianity. Too many of us imagine that Christ means to us nothing more than the possession of negative goodness. Multitudes of people have the idea that Christianity is nothing more than a virtuous way of living. If this were true, Christianity would be cold and negative, joyless, unadventurous, a retreat from the world, completely lacking as a changing force in society. In its true meaning Christianity is a God-centered way of living, an adventure in faith, a companionship with Christ, a sharing with Him His passion for humanity and His mission of redemption, a battle, a victory—the victory of faith that overcomes the world and presses on to the conquest of the world for Christ and His kingdom.

It is not enough to be good, we must be good soldiers. We must be confident of victory, but we must not expect an easy victory. Christ said to His disciples: "Fear not, little flock; for it is your Father's good pleasure to give you the kingdom." But He also warned them: "Men will lay hands on you and persecute you, handing you over to synagogues and prisons; you will be dragged before kings and governors for the sake of my name." These were the twelve Jesus had chosen to carry His message in a hostile world. At first they were afraid, and they had every reason to be. But after their great baptism of fire they feared no man. Once they got started they wore the badge of courage to the end.

Someone has written: "Faith is not belief in spite of evidence, but life in scorn of consequences." Such faith and fear do not go together. The men of the New Testament, although outnumbered by a great pagan world, had the kingdom of God in their hearts and a great confidence in the certainty of its triumph.

They were sure of themselves, and their message. And it was no hallucination of disordered minds that made them so confident that the weapons of the Spirit could cast down the strongholds of paganism. And because of this, Glover, the historian, could commit himself to print, unafraid of contradiction, declaring that "the early Christian outthought, outlived, and outdid the pagan."

Say what you like, there was no fear, no cowardice, no defeatist spirit among the first-century Christians. They were but a small handful. They had no standing, and most of them were poor. But they backed Christ and His truth against current error. Everywhere they proclaimed His message in scorn of consequences. Today we, their successors, need this same forthright courage to face the pagan powers and other forces hostile to Christ and Christendom. Heaven forbid that we should interpret Christian meekness to be weakness. In this battle of Christendom any show of weakness would be fatal. We are called to stand upon our feet and hold ourselves with manly dignity and courage in a world where spiritual values are scorned. The battle may be hard, but there is Jude's appeal trumpeted to us across the centuries, "*Go on strongly fighting for the faith!*"

27

Able to Keep You

> "Now unto him that is able to keep you from falling, and to present you faultless before the presence of his glory with exceeding joy, to the only wise God our Saviour, be glory and majesty, dominion and power, both now and ever. Amen."—*Jude 24-25*.

How shall we guard ourselves against apostasy and its evil effects? How shall we be kept true to the faith in the face of the forces which seek to destroy it? How shall we keep our ideals and live worthy lives in the midst of the ungodly atmosphere created by apostate and antichrist forces ? The answer is in the doxology with which Jude ends his epistle. "Now to him who is able to keep you from slipping and to make you stand unblemished and exultant before his glory—to the only God, our Saviour through Jesus Christ our Lord, be glory, majesty, dominion and authority, before all time and now and for all time: Amen." He is the One in whom our faith is centered—"Jesus Christ the same, yesterday, today and for ever." To have our faith centered in Him, is our stay against "being carried away with a variety of novel doctrines" (Hebrews 13:8-9).

Through nineteen centuries Jesus Christ has remained the joy of loving hearts, the hope and comfort of trusting souls, the life and light of believing men and women, the source and center of the Christian movement. No man or church that made Jesus Christ the center was ever known to come off the worse in any circumstances or in any encounter. This is not just a religious platitude. It is the simple fact, attested by generation after generation.

The circumference of the Christian movement has sometimes been broken into by paganism. Unbelief and infidelity have taken a toll of its outer lines. Some of its outward forms have broken down under the impact of change. But nobody has ever been able to detect any weakness in the center—Jesus Christ the same, yesterday, today, and forever.

The question for every church, for every individual Christian, is the same: What have you got at the center? If all we have there is ourselves, active and good-intentioned though we may be, we shall fail. It was Francis Bacon who said, "It is a poor center of a man's actions, himself." That is true of any social activity. It is particularly true of activity in religion. In the Christian realm, Christ must be at the center of our life and activity if we are to live triumphantly and be really dynamic for service. We shall never fail if we keep Christ at the center of our lives and activities, so that we are able to say with Paul, "I live, yet not I, but Christ liveth in me." It is in Him that our faith is centered. We must live by confidence in Him. As Jude counsels, we must build up ourselves in this holy faith and pray in the Holy Spirit, so keeping ourselves within the love of God and waiting for the mercy of our Lord Jesus Christ that ends in life eternal. Let us do this, and the doxology of this epistle shall be our song of victory. And at the end, when we pass from the scenes of this transient world and appear amidst the scenes of the eternal world beyond, this song of our earthly pilgrimage will be merged with the song of that "great host whom no one can count, from every nation and tribe and people and tongue, standing before the throne and before the Lamb, clad in white robes, with palm-branches in their hands, [singing] with a loud voice: 'Saved by our God who is seated on the throne, and by the Lamb! . . . Even so! Blessing and glory and wisdom and thanksgiving and honour and power and might be to our God for ever and ever: Amen!' " (Revelation 7:9-11, 12, Moffatt).

28

What Lies Beyond?

"On the Lord's day I found myself rapt in the Spirit, and I heard a loud voice behind me like a trumpet calling, 'Write your vision in a book' "

—*Revelation 1:10-11 (Moffatt).*

There on the lonely isle of Patmos the mystic apostle had been making, as it were, a reconnaissance, investigating the claims of the Christian faith with regard to the spiritual world—the world beyond. Was that world a reality? Would it fulfill the Christian hope? And then, on the Lord's day, rapt in the Spirit, he was lifted up to a height far above the earth level where he saw and heard things that were never seen and heard by the natural eye and ear. In the Book of Revelation he reports what he saw and heard. For the moment, we are concerned, not so much with the details of his report, but with the conception it conveys, namely, that beyond this mundane sphere there is a realm of living spiritual beings, that life in that realm is not only a reality but perfect in its completeness and glorious in its fullness.

Look at some of the scenes he reports:

"Then I heard a voice from heaven saying, 'Write this: "Blessed are the dead who die in the Lord from henceforth! Even so—it is the voice of the Spirit; let them rest from their toils; for what they have done goes with them" ' " (14:13, Moffatt).

"Then I looked, and there was a white cloud, and seated on the cloud One resembling a human being" (14:14a, Moffatt).

"Then I heard a cry like the shout of a great host . . . 'Hallelujah! now the Lord our God almighty reigns! Let us rejoice and triumph, let us give him the glory!' " (19:6-7, Moffatt).

Here was something more than the fancies of a dreaming mystic. Here was divine revelation —the revelation of reality. The apostle John was wide awake, not dreaming. The voice he heard was a loud voice, like a trumpet calling —no mistaking it.

You may be sure of this, that what we see in this mundane sphere is but a small part of what there is to see. Beyond the frontiers of sight and sense lie the vast regions of a spiritual order infinite in its reaches and inexhaustible in its riches. Faith is a reconnaissance from a height far above the level of our other means of investigation, and nothing that it discovers is more certain than its report of another world of teeming life beyond this mortal sphere. Much of what is there must seem puzzling from this side, and many of our eager questions must go unanswered. But there is no rightful expectation we can have toward that spiritual world that it will not fulfill.

In all ages men have believed that in this life we are at the beginning and not the end of our experiences. Through the ages men have asked, and are still asking: Whither do I go when I leave this world? What will I be? After I finish my few years of struggling and striving on this planet, whither shall I go, what will become of me then, what will become of my thinking faculty, the soul, when I shed this earthly body?

No human intelligence can supply a complete answer to these questions. But to the people of Christian faith, what the apostle John says is a satisfying answer: "It doth not yet appear what we shall be: but we know that, when he shall appear, we shall be like him; for we shall see him as he is" (1 John 3:2). And then there is Paul's view. He speaks of the seed you sow in the ground. "What you sow," he says, "is not the body that is to be; it is a mere grain of wheat, or some other seed. God gives it a body as he pleases, gives each kind of seed a body of its own." "So with the resurrection of the dead," he continues: "what is sown is mortal, what rises is immortal; sown inglorious, it rises in glory, sown in weakness, it rises in power; sown an animate body, it rises a spiritual body" (1 Corinthians 15:37-38, 42-44, Moffatt).

How often we have listened at the graveside to those words, "ashes to ashes, dust to dust." Is that the last word? No, says the Christian faith. Out of those ashes and dust will spring a new body—a miracle of grace and glory.

29

Faithfulness the Crown of Life

"Be thou faithful unto death, and I will give thee a crown of life."—*Revelation 2:10.*

I am glad the text does not read, Be thou brilliant; or, Be thou eloquent; or, Be thou successful. I am glad it does not say, Be thou a great preacher; or, Be thou a great writer; or, Be thou a great statesman. If it said any of these things, most of us could never hope to attain the crown of life which it promises.

All that God wants of anyone is faithfulness. Not brilliance, not eloquence, not success, not eminence, not notoriety which attracts newspaper notice, but the quiet, regular, faithful performance of duty in our appointed place—that is the thing that attracts the eye of God, and that is the thing He promises to reward with the crown of life. God crowns men for being faithful, not for being great preachers, or great writers, or great statesmen.

Not many of us are endowed with brilliant intellect. Not many of us can hope to achieve high position and renown. Most of us belong in the rank and file, and will never attract much of the world's attention. There are many of us who are destined never to win notable success in a worldly way. We cannot all be men of affairs. Most of the jobs in this world are small jobs. But whatever our limitations, however small the place we fill, we can be faithful. To be faithful, we do not need to be geniuses, and we do not need the world's acclaim. The man the world acclaims is not always the one God acclaims. God says, "He that is faithful in that which is least is faithful also in much." To be faithful in that which is least will win as rich a reward as faithfulness in the greatest.

There is something better than occupying high station, and having one's every act chronicled by admiring pens. That something better is to be faithful. Not genius, not fame, but faithfulness is the crowning glory of life.

30

On to the City of God

"I saw a new heaven and a new earth . . . the holy city . . . coming down from God."—*Revelation 21:1, 2.*

The world is greatly indebted to its far-seeing men like John who had the vision to see in the distant future a new earth and a holy city. Glance back through the centuries and you will find that all the world's great torchbearers, leaders, and benefactors were such men. They were men inspired by motives drawn from a far-off future. The presence of such men in the world has kept human society buoyant and hopeful.

With so much war and carnage and death and destruction going on, with so much turmoil and strife, with so many turbulent voices speaking different things, with clashing interests and conflicting ambitions playing havoc everywhere, it would seem that this is a hopeless world. But thank God for a faith which refuses to accept this apparently hopeless situation, which is able to construct out of the present disorder a new world wherein righteousness shall reign and all mankind shall know the blessedness of peace and good will.

In point of time we may yet be further away from paradise restored than from paradise lost, but through the vision of faith the distant ideal comes enchantingly and hopefully near. It is true, there are many so lacking in faith that they have never caught the glorious vision. Groveling in the dust of despair, they shake their heads doubtfully and say, "It is all too vague"; while they of a cynical spirit protest against disturbing things as they are, saying, "What's the use? If men want to do wrong and women don't want to do right, it can't be helped; society must have its redeeming vices; all things are subject to compromise; we can never have a perfect social order." But in the presence of such pessimism the man of true faith in the great realities of divine truth is enabled to keep his eye fixed on the morning star of hope as he presses

> On to the boundless waste
> On to the city of God.